PRAXIS® 5004 Social Studies Elementary Education
PRAXIS® II – Elementary Education Multiple Subjects Exam 5001
By: Preparing Teachers In America™

This page is intentionally left blank.

This page is intentionally left blank.

Free Online Email Tutoring Services

All preparation guides purchased directly from Preparing Teachers In America includes a free three month email tutoring subscription. Any resale of preparation guides does not qualify for a free email tutoring subscription.

What is Email Tutoring?

Email Tutoring allows buyers to send questions to tutors via email. Buyers can send any questions regarding the exam processes, strategies, content questions, or practice questions. Preparing Teachers In America reserves the right not to answer questions with or without reason(s).

How to use Email Tutoring?

Buyers need to send an email to onlinepreparationservices@gmail.com requesting email tutoring services. Buyers may be required to confirm the email address used to purchase the preparation guide or additional information prior to using email tutoring. Once email tutoring subscription is confirmed, buyers will be provided an email address to send questions to. The three month period will start the day the subscription is confirmed.

Any misuse of email tutoring services will result in termination of service. Preparing Teachers In America reserves the right to terminate email tutoring subscription at anytime with or without notice.

Comments and Suggestions

All comments and suggestions for improvements for the study guide and email tutoring services need to be sent to onlinepreparationservices@gmail.com.

This page is intentionally left blank.

Table of Content

This page is intentionally left blank.

About the Exam and Study Guide

What is the PRAXIS 5004 Elementary Education Social Studies Exam?

The PRAXIS 5004 Elementary Education Social Studies is an exam to test potential teachers' competencies in basic social studies skills necessary to pursue a teaching career in elementary education. The exam is aligned with the Common Core State Standards, and the exam covers the following content areas:
- United States History
- Government and Citizenship
- World History
- Economics
- Geography, Anthropology, and Sociology

The exam is timed at 50 minutes and consists of 55 questions. The 55 selected-response questions are based on knowledge obtained in a bachelor's degree program. The exam contains some questions that may not count toward the score.

What topics are covered on the exam?

The following are some topics covered on the exam:
- European exploration and colonization
- American Revolution
- Westward expansion, industrialization, Great Depression
- Nature, purpose, and forms of government
- Rights and responsibilities of citizenship in a democracy
- Connections between causes and effects of events
- United States, Constitution, Declaration of Independence, and Gettysburg Address
- World and regional geography
- Major contributions of classical civilizations
- Economics affects population, resources, and technology
- Apply geography to interpret past, to interpret present, and to plan for future
- Twentieth-century developments and transformations in world history
- Supply and demand, scarcity, and choice, money and resources

What is included in this study guide book?

This guide includes two full length practice exams for the PRAXIS 5004 Elementary Education Social Studies Exam along with detail explanations. The recommendation is to take the exams under exam conditions of 50 minutes and a quiet environment.

This page is intentionally left blank.

Practice Test 1

This page is intentionally left blank.

Exam Answer Sheet Test 1

Below is an optional answer sheet to use to document answers.

Question Number	Selected Answer	Question Number	Selected Answer
1		29	
2		30	
3		31	
4		32	
5		33	
6		34	
7		35	
8		36	
9		37	
10		38	
11		39	
12		40	
13		41	
14		42	
15		43	
16		44	
17		45	
18		46	
19		47	
20		48	
21		49	
22		50	
23		51	
24		52	
25		53	
26		54	
27		55	
28			

This page is intentionally left blank.

QUESTION 1

Who was the first woman to contribute to women's right to vote?

  A. Eleanor Roosevelt
  B. Susan B. Anthony
  C. Elizabeth Cady Stanton
  D. Rosa Parks

 Answer:

QUESTION 2

What mountain range has Mt. Everest?

  A. Himalaya
  B. Andes
  C. Appalachian
  D. Danley Hill

 Answer:

QUESTION 3

Which of the following best explains the importance of the Montgomery bus boycott of 1955?

  A. sparked the revolution for black women's equal rights
  B. showed the effectiveness of direct, nonviolent resistance
  C. showed Americans that black lives were important
  D. sparked civil rights leaders to take rigorous action to initiate voter registration campaigns

 Answer:

QUESTION 4

The _____ is an amendment that provided limited protection of lands conveyed on the behalf of Alaska Natives to for-profit corporations.

  A. Alaska Native Claims Settlement Act of 1971
  B. Alaska Protection Plan of 1991
  C. Land Ownership Act of 1981
  D. Alaska Constitution

Answer:

QUESTION 5

The origins of the Cold War can be linked to United States-Soviet Union differences regarding which of the following postwar questions?

  A. How much land should the Soviet Union hold in the region?
  B. What form of government should be implemented in Eastern Europe?
  C. How much power the United States should have in resolving conflicts with Soviet Union?
  D. What organizations should be started to reform trading with Soviet Union?

Answer:

QUESTION 6

Encouraging African Americans to fight for the Union, strengthening the Union militarily, and shifting the focus of the war to freedom for all are linked to which of the following?

  A. President Lincoln's First Inaugural Address
  B. The Declaration of Independence
  C. The Emancipation Proclamation
  D. The Fourteenth Amendment

Answer:

QUESTION 7

Which of the following best describes the significance of the decision in Marbury vs. Madison in American history?

    A. ended racial discrimination in schools across America
    B. established the practice of judicial review by the Supreme Court
    C. confirmed the power of Congress to be involved in international trade
    D. upheld the power of the people to choose the vice president

Answer:

QUESTION 8

"The President…shall have Power, by and with the Advice and Consent of the Senate, to make Treaties, provided two thirds of the Senators concurs." – United States Constitution, Article II, Section 2

The excerpt above provides an example of which constitutional principal?

    A. checks and balances
    B. popular sovereignty
    C. individual rights
    D. federalism

Answer:

QUESTION 9

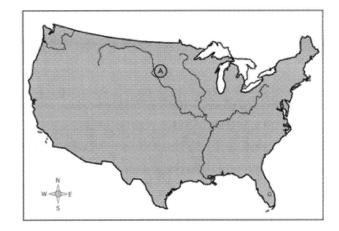

The river identified as letter A on this map played a major role in

    A. at the Battle of Saratoga
    B. the American Revolution
    C. the Civil War
    D. the exploration of territory obtained from France

Answer:

QUESTION 10

Which of the following is the best example of cultural diffusion?

    A. ancient Rome's contribution of democracy
    B. Buddhism spread from India to China
    C. gunpowder originated in India and eventually came to Europe
    D. overthrow of Mongol and creation of Ming Dynasty

Answer:

QUESTION 11

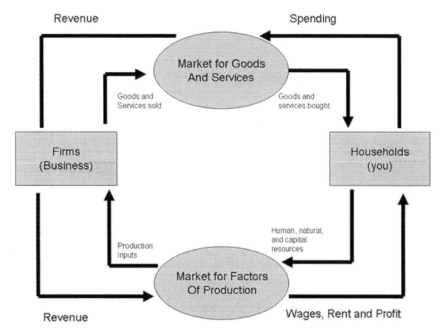

Which of the following economies is shown in the image above?

    A. command economic system
    B. mixed economy
    C. market economy
    D. pure economy

Answer:

QUESTION 12

At the outbreak of both World War I and World War II in Europe, public opinion in the United States generally favored which of the following?

    A. remaining neutral
    B. entering the war for brief period
    C. not entering the war unless America was directly impacted
    D. using international peace organization to resolve conflict

Answer:

QUESTION 13

The United States Senate and the House of Representatives has passed a legislation. However, the President vetoes the legislation. Under what requirement can the legislation still become a law?

    A. the vice president provides approval
    B. at least two-thirds of both houses of Congress agree
    C. at least five members of the Supreme Court ruling to pass legislation
    D. voters agree to the legislation during election year

Answer:

QUESTION 14

Which of the following best describes the opportunity cost of a good?

    A. the time incurred in finding it
    B. the number of other goods sacrificed to obtain another unit of that good
    C. the number of other goods gained to obtain another unit of a different good
    D. the loss of interest in using savings

Answer:

QUESTION 15

In all economic system, scarcity imposes limitations on

    A. households, governments, business firms, and the nation as a whole
    B. households and business firms, but not the governments
    C. households and governments, but not business firms
    D. business firms, governments, and the nation as a whole

Answer:

QUESTION 16

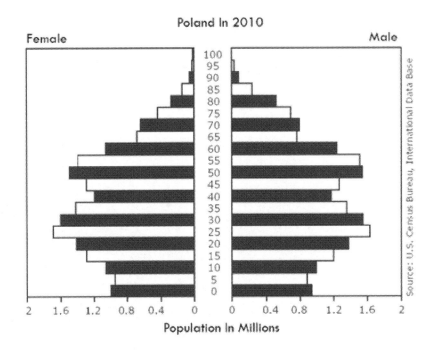

Poland In 2010

Female   Male

Population In Millions

Source: U.S. Census Bureau, International Data Base

Which is a possible conclusion about Poland based on the population pyramid?

    A. The demand for elderly care services will go up.

    B. Equal pay for equal work for women will be a greater issue in coming years.

    C. Individuals will spend less money on prenatal care in 30 years.

    D. Public education will see a shortage of teachers in 10 years.

Answer:

QUESTION 17

Source: Herblock, *The Washington Post*, June 18, 1963

The above cartoon is expressing public reaction on what decision made by the Supreme Court?

    A. school-sponsored prayer declared unconstitutional
    B. banned the pledge from public educational institution
    C. placed limitation on church attendees
    D. recommended home-base prayers

Answer:

QUESTION 18

I. Federal Reserve Bank system is made up of 12 regional banks, the Board of Governors of the Federal Reserve System, and the Federal Open Market Committee.

II. Federal Reserve Banks are located in San Francisco, Atlanta, and Kansas City.

III. Federal Reserve Banks functions are to issue new currency, hold deposits for the banks in their districts, and operate the payments network.

Of the above, which of the following is/are accurate?

A. III only
B. I and II
C. II and III
D. I, II, and III

Answer:

QUESTION 19

Which of the following best describes the difference of the public sector from the private sector?

A. it is paid by various tax arrangements
B. it provides public services
C. it conducts official elections
D. it is controlled by a political framework

Answer:

QUESTION 20

What is the length of a term for a United States Senator?

A. 2 years
B. 4 years
C. 6 years
D. 8 years

Answer:

QUESTION 21

When national output rises, the economy is said to be in

    A. an inflation
    B. an expansion
    C. a deflation
    D. a recession

Answer:

QUESTION 22

Which of the following beliefs did the Ancient Greeks and the modern United States share?

    A. laws are critical to ensure societies remain stable
    B. leaders should be chosen by political parties
    C. buildings should not have columns
    D. certain groups should not vote

Answer:

QUESTION 23

Column A lists theoretical models of economic organizations and Column B lists their major strength. Which of the following is the best match?

Letter	Column A	Column B
A	Command	is less likely than other economic systems to have problems related to scarcity
B	Mixed	combines the economic productivity of a market system with the distributional efficiency of a command system
C	Traditional	is more likely than other economic systems to use democratic procedures to make basic economic decisions
D	Market	provides a strong basis for the expression of state-based initiatives

Answer:

QUESTION 24

Which of the following best describes how the United States' democracy differs from democracy in Athens, Greece?

    A. Individuals in United States democracy vote depending on race.
    B. Democracy in the United States is only used during election season.
    C. People in the United States directly vote on which laws are implemented.
    D. The United States elects representatives as oppose to voting on laws directly.

Answer:

QUESTION 25

Which of the following significantly contributed to the fall of the Roman Empire?

    A. individuals' refusal to participate in the democratic process
    B. a period of excessive disorder and a weak national government
    C. growth of surrounding countries
    D. excessive national debt

Answer:

QUESTION 26

In World War II, which two cities were destroyed by atomic bombs before Japan agreed to surrender?

    A. Tokyo and Hiroshima
    B. Nagasaki and Shanghai
    C. Hiroshima and Nagasaki
    D. Nagasaki and Tokyo

Answer:

QUESTION 27

What was a major effect of World War II on women and minorities in the United States?

    A. increased opportunities in the workplace
    B. equal pay for equal work for all individuals
    C. increased participation in democratic process
    D. selective service requirements extended to women and minorities

Answer:

QUESTION 28

     I.   lithosphere --- landforms
     II.   hydrosphere ---water features
     III.   biosphere --- nature

Of the above, which of the following is/are correctly matched?
    A. I only
    B. II only
    C. I and II
    D. I, II, and III

Answer:

QUESTION 29

The United States Constitution guarantees the right to a writ of habeas corpus. The main reason for this was to

    A. to prevent the illegal imprisonment of individual in the United States.
    B. to prevent illegal arrests.
    C. to prevent search of homes without warrants.
    D. to give individuals the right to a speedy trail.

Answer:

QUESTION 30

    I.   Bill of Rights
    II.   Articles of Confederation
    III.   Declaration of Independence
    IV.   United States Constitution

Which of the following correctly orders the above documents starting from the first written?

    A. II, I, III, IV
    B. III, II, IV, I
    C. III, II, I, IV
    D. I, II, IV, III

Answer:

QUESTION 31

Draining of the Everglades has been done primarily for:

    A.   urban development
    B.   economic development
    C.   government development
    D.   social development

Answer:

QUESTION 32

Individuals who lead and supported the Chinese Revolution of 1949 broke mainly with the Chinese past in their:

    A. creation of a Paleolithic, centralized state
    B. culture of remaining isolated
    C. stress on class conflict, science, and materialism
    D. ability to increase exports

Answer:

QUESTION 33

The State of Rhode Island can be best used for measuring which of the following?

    A.   City of St. Petersburg, Florida
    B.   State of Texas
    C.   State of Delaware
    D.   City of Indianapolis, Indiana

Answer:

QUESTION 34

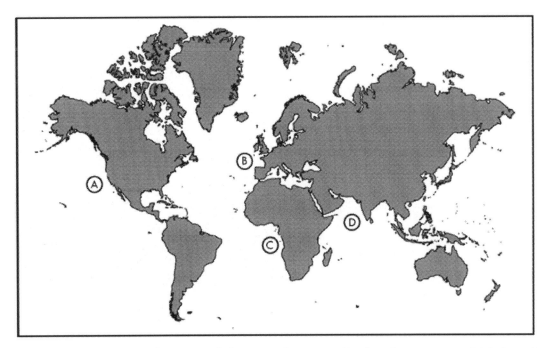

Merchants use monsoon winds to travel along trade routes. In the above map, which location did merchants historically use?

A. A
B. B
C. C
D. D

Answer:

QUESTION 35

The United States government and the state governments share responsibilities of _____.

    A. declaring schools unfit
    B. operating post offices
    C. conducting elections
    D. establishing courts

Answer:

QUESTION 36

The following are groups within a local police department:

    I.   street patrol
    II.   detective work
    III.   domestic cases
    IV.   traffic control

The organizational structure is a reflection of which economic concept:

    A. division of labor
    B. opportunity cost
    C. organization
    D. economic efficiency

Answer:

QUESTION 37

Which of the following was the main reason for replacing the Articles of Confederation with the United States Constitution?

    A. limited the power of the national government
    B. expand the powers of the national government
    C. decreased the autonomy of state and local government
    D. made the government more accountable for the people

Answer:

QUESTION 38

A circular model shows what feature of a market economy?

    A. exchange of goods and services
    B. exchange of hazards
    C. global model
    D. no opportunity cost involved

Answer:

QUESTION 39

In the latter part of the nineteenth century, the United States agricultural business in the Midwest started to transform from a market system of small family farms to one dominated by large commercialized farms. This change is mostly due to:

    A. the increasing population density in the region
    B. the technological advances in railroad transportation
    C. the posts Cold War impact
    D. the increase in exports of agricultural resources

Answer:

QUESTION 40

To better understand the impact of ancient Greece on the historical development of Western civilization, the best resources to examine are related to:
    A. increase of absolute monarchies
    B. causes of the Reformation
    C. emergence of feudalism
    D. origins of the Renaissance

Answer:

QUESTION 41

In the United States, local governments normally use a significant amount of their resources to:

    A. give mental health services
    B. impose environmental regulations
    C. provide elementary and secondary schools programs
    D. develop outside art structures

Answer:

QUESTION 42

A topographic map is best used for:

    A. determining the difference in elevation between a river and a close by mountain range
    B. knowing the types of coastal landforms found in a region
    C. locating the shortest route between two places
    D. comparing the population distribution of two states

Answer:

.

QUESTION 43

_____ is the process by which a person or group language/culture comes to resemble those of another group.

    A. assimilation
    B. diffusion
    C. syncretism
    D. resemblance

Answer:

QUESTION 44

Which of the following is best related to the principle of popular sovereignty guaranteed by the U.S. Constitution?

    A. "All courts shall be open, and every person, for an injury done to him in his person, property or reputation, shall have remedy by due course of law."
    B. "Every citizen may freely speak, write and publish his sentiments on all subjects, being responsible for the abuse of that liberty."
    C. "The people shall be secure in their persons, houses, papers and possessions from unreasonable searches or seizures."
    D. "All political power is inherent in the people . . . and they have at all times an undeniable and indefeasible right to alter their form of government in such manner as they may think expedient."

Answer:

QUESTION 45

Which of the following was a major impact of World War I?

    A. the onset of economic depression in America
    B. the rise of nationalist movements in the Austro-Hungarian empire
    C. the rise of communism in Russia
    D. the limited number of jobs in America

Answer:

QUESTION 46

Under international law, which of the following is a violation of human rights?

    A. a prisoner arrested is not allowed to communicate with family members
    B. a refugee is unable to obtain work in the host country
    C. a teenager is not allowed to travel to his parents' home country
    D. an individual arrested without being given his/her Miranda rights

Answer:

QUESTION 47

Which of the following is a difference in the way a democratic and authoritarian government operates?

    A. the selection of government leaders
    B. having a governing document
    C. the currency system
    D. the enforcement of law

Answer:

QUESTION 48

Which of the following provides the basic reason for the support of public education in the United States?

    A. skilled labor
    B. trained professors
    C. informed citizens
    D. educated leaders

Answer:

QUESTION 49

The Napoleonic Code was a

    A. military strategy
    B. legal system
    C. political system
    D. behavioral system

Answer:

QUESTION 50

Which of the following is an inaccurate statement?

    A. all taxes and other revenues exceed government expenditures for a year is called a budget surplus

    B. revenues and expenditures are equal during a given period is called a balanced budget

    C. expenditures exceed revenue from taxes is called a cyclical crisis.

    D. actual dollar expenditures, revenues, and deficits in a given period is called an actual budget

Answer:

QUESTION 51

Zora Neale Hurston and Langston Hughes were a part of what period in American history?

    A. Harlem Renaissance

    B. Restoration Age

    C. Old English

    D. Victorian literature

Answer:

QUESTION 52

A change from a direct democracy to a representative democracy is best undertaken when

    A. economic status of people change for the better.

    B. nations acquire additional land.

    C. population increases.

    D. many individuals are not voting.

Answer:

QUESTION 53

After World War II, the United States had a program that provided money, supplies, and machinery to assist European counties in rebuilding. What was the program called?

A. Marshall Plan
B. Four Point Program
C. Truman Doctrine
D. New Deal

Answer:

QUESTION 54

Which of the following is most critical for a historical researcher to consider when reading through resources on individuals being interviewed on the impact of the Great Depression had on the State in 1970?

A. individuals say what they think the interviewer wants to hear
B. individuals don't understand the impact it had on history
C. individuals minds have changed over the years
D. individuals location at the time

Answer:

QUESTION 55

Population and Square Miles of Countries

Country	Land in square miles	Population in millions
Israel	7550	5.4
Iraq	168860	19.2
Jordan	34340	3.6
Kuwait	7102	1.7

According to the above data, which country is the most densely populated?

A. Iraq113
B. Jordan 104
C. Israel 715
D. Kuwait 239

Answer:

Answer Key Test 1

Question Number	Correct Answer	Question Number	Correct Answer
1	C	29	A
2	A	30	B
3	B	31	A
4	B	32	C
5	B	33	B
6	C	34	D
7	B	35	D
8	A	36	A
9	D	37	B
10	B	38	A
11	C	39	B
12	A	40	D
13	B	41	C
14	B	42	A
15	A	43	A
16	A	44	D
17	A	45	A
18	D	46	A
19	D	47	A
20	C	48	C
21	B	49	B
22	A	50	C
23	A	51	A
24	D	52	C
25	B	53	A
26	C	54	B
27	A	55	C
28	D		

NOTE: Getting approximately 80% of the questions correct increases chances of obtaining passing score on the real exam. This varies from different states and university programs.

This page is intentionally left blank.

Elementary Education – Social Studies Questions And Answers – Test 1
55 Questions

QUESTION 1

Who was the first woman to contribute to women's right to vote?

    A. Eleanor Roosevelt
    B. Susan B. Anthony
    C. Elizabeth Cady Stanton
    D. Rosa Parks

Answer: C

Explanation: Elizabeth Cady Stanton was an early leader of the woman's rights movement. She held the Seneca Falls Convention in July 1848 where she took the lead in proposing that women be granted the right to vote.

QUESTION 2

What mountain range has Mt. Everest?

    A. Himalaya
    B. Andes
    C. Appalachian
    D. Danley Hill

Answer: A

Explanation: Mount Everest is part of the Himalaya mountain range along the border of Nepal and Tibet.

QUESTION 3

Which of the following best explains the importance of the Montgomery bus boycott of 1955?

  A. sparked the revolution for black women's equal rights
  B. showed the effectiveness of direct, nonviolent resistance
  C. showed Americans that black lives were important
  D. sparked civil rights leaders to take rigorous action to initiate voter registration campaigns

Answer: B

Explanation: Montgomery bus boycott resulted in the arrest of Rosa Parks. The Montgomery bus boycott was a 13-month mass protest that ended with the United States Supreme Court ruling that segregation on public buses is unconstitutional. The bus boycott showed the potential for nonviolent mass protest to successfully challenge racial segregation.

QUESTION 4

The _____ is an amendment that provided limited protection of lands conveyed on the behalf of Alaska Natives to for-profit corporations.

  A. Alaska Native Claims Settlement Act of 1971
  B. Alaska Protection Plan of 1991
  C. Land Ownership Act of 1981
  D. Alaska Constitution

Answer: B

Explanation: The Alaska Protection Plan of 1991 is an amendment that provided limited protection of lands conveyed on the behalf of Alaska Natives to for-profit corporations.

QUESTION 5

The origins of the Cold War can be linked to United States-Soviet Union differences regarding which of the following postwar questions?

  A. How much land should the Soviet Union hold in the region?
  B. What form of government should be implemented in Eastern Europe?
  C. How much power the United States should have in resolving conflicts with Soviet Union?
  D. What organizations should be started to reform trading with Soviet Union?

Answer: B

Explanation: The Cold War was a state of political and military tension after World War II between powers in the Western Bloc and powers in the Eastern Bloc. The United States-Soviet Union differed on the type of government that should be formed in Eastern Europe.

QUESTION 6

Encouraging African Americans to fight for the Union, strengthening the Union militarily, and shifting the focus of the war to freedom for all are linked to which of the following?

  A. President Lincoln's First Inaugural Address
  B. The Declaration of Independence
  C. The Emancipation Proclamation
  D. The Fourteenth Amendment

Answer: C

Explanation: The Emancipation Proclamation stated "that all persons held as slaves" within the rebellious states "are, and henceforward shall be free." As a result, this encouraged African Americans to fight for the Union, strengthening the Union militarily, and shifting the focus of the war to freedom for all.

QUESTION 7

Which of the following best describes the significance of the decision in Marbury vs. Madison in American history?

    A. ended racial discrimination in schools across America
    B. established the practice of judicial review by the Supreme Court
    C. confirmed the power of Congress to be involved in international trade
    D. upheld the power of the people to choose the vice president

Answer: B

Explanation: This was the ruling that established a precedent for judicial review in the United States. It declared that acts of Congress that conflict with the Constitution are null in void, as the constitution is the highest law of the land.

QUESTION 8

"The President…shall have Power, by and with the Advice and Consent of the Senate, to make Treaties, provided two thirds of the Senators concurs." – United States Constitution, Article II, Section 2

The excerpt above provides an example of which constitutional principal?

    A. checks and balances
    B. popular sovereignty
    C. individual rights
    D. federalism

Answer: A

Explanation: Checks and balances is when each branch of the government has some measure of influence over the other branches and may choose to block procedures of the other branches. The statement indicates the President has to obtain consent from the Senate to make treaties; this is an example of checks and balances.

QUESTION 9

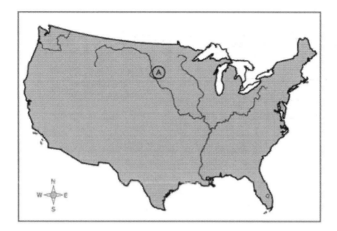

The river identified as letter A on this map played a major role in

A. at the Battle of Saratoga
B. the American Revolution
C. the Civil War
D. the exploration of territory obtained from France

Answer: D

Explanation: Letter A represents the Missouri River, which was major role in the exploration of territory obtained from France.

QUESTION 10

Which of the following is the best example of cultural diffusion?

A. ancient Rome's contribution of democracy
B. Buddhism spread from India to China
C. gunpowder originated in India and eventually came to Europe
D. overthrow of Mongol and creation of Ming Dynasty

Answer: B

Explanation: Culture diffusion is the spreading out of culture, culture traits, or a cultural pattern from a central point. Buddhism (which has particular aspects of culture) were spread to other regions, such as India or China.

QUESTION 11

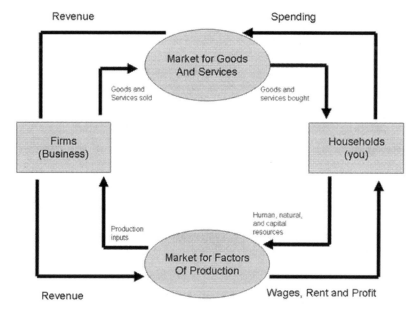

Which of the following economies is shown in the image above?

A. command economic system
B. mixed economy
C. market economy
D. pure economy

Answer: C

Explanation: The image shows a market economy, which is a when decisions regarding investment, production, and distribution are based on market determined supply and demand.

QUESTION 12

At the outbreak of both World War I and World War II in Europe, public opinion in the United States generally favored which of the following?

    A. remaining neutral
    B. entering the war for brief period
    C. not entering the war unless America was directly impacted
    D. using international peace organization to resolve conflict

Answer: A

Explanation: Majority of Americans were in favor of remaining neutral during the outbreak of both World War I and World War II in Europe. This was so that American military men would not have to go to war or to prevent the United States from incurring significant cost.

QUESTION 13

The United States Senate and the House of Representatives has passed a legislation. However, the President vetoes the legislation. Under what requirement can the legislation still become a law?

    A. the vice president provides approval
    B. at least two-thirds of both houses of Congress agree
    C. at least five members of the Supreme Court ruling to pass legislation
    D. voters agree to the legislation during election year

Answer: B

Explanation: If two-thirds of both houses of Congress vote to enact a bill following a presidential veto, the legislation becomes a law. This is expressed under Article I, Section 7 of the United States Constitution.

QUESTION 14

Which of the following best describes the opportunity cost of a good?

    A. the time incurred in finding it
    B. the number of other goods sacrificed to obtain another unit of that good
    C. the number of other goods gained to obtain another unit of a different good
    D. the loss of interest in using savings

Answer: B

Explanation: Opportunity cost is a benefit, profit, or value of something that must be given up to acquire or achieve something else.

QUESTION 15

In all economic system, scarcity imposes limitations on

    A. households, governments, business firms, and the nation as a whole
    B. households and business firms, but not the governments
    C. households and governments, but not business firms
    D. business firms, governments, and the nation as a whole

Answer: A

Explanation: Economic impacts related to scarcity impose limitations households, governments, business firms, and the nation as a whole. In other words, no one is immune to scarcity.

QUESTION 16

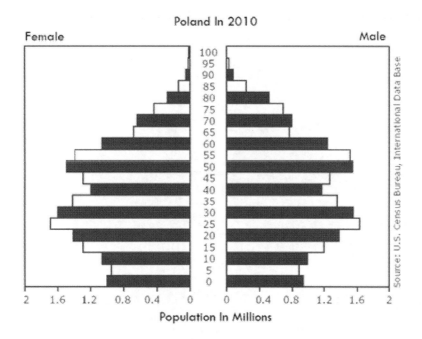

Poland In 2010

Female   Male

Population In Millions

Source: U.S. Census Bureau, International Data Base

Which is a possible conclusion about Poland based on the population pyramid?

    A. The demand for elderly care services will go up.
    B. Equal pay for equal work for women will be a greater issue in coming years.
    C. Individuals will spend less money on prenatal care in 30 years.
    D. Public education will see a shortage of teachers in 10 years.

Answer: A

Explanation: This is a population pyramid, so the middle column in the population pyramid is the age. The population for individuals above age 60 is very high, which indicates there is going to be a demand for care services for the elderly. The other answer choices cannot be concluded based on the information provided in the population pyramid.

QUESTION 17

Source: Herblock, *The Washington Post,* June 18, 1963

The above cartoon is expressing public reaction on what decision made by the Supreme Court?

    A. school-sponsored prayer declared unconstitutional
    B. banned the pledge from public educational institution
    C. placed limitation on church attendees
    D. recommended home-base prayers

Answer: A

Explanation: Engel v. Vitale was a landmark United States Supreme Court case that determined that it is unconstitutional for state officials to compose an official school prayer and encourage its recitation in public schools.

QUESTION 18

I.   Federal Reserve Bank system is made up of 12 regional banks, the Board of Governors of the Federal Reserve System, and the Federal Open Market Committee.

II.   Federal Reserve Banks are located in San Francisco, Atlanta, and Kansas City.

III.   Federal Reserve Banks functions are to issue new currency, hold deposits for the banks in their districts, and operate the payments network.

Of the above, which of the following is/are accurate?

A. III only
B. I and II
C. II and III
D. I, II, and III

Answer: D

Explanation: All statements are accurate regarding the Federal Reserve Banks.

QUESTION 19

Which of the following best describes the difference of the public sector from the private sector?

   A. it is paid by various tax arrangements
   B. it provides public services
   C. it conducts official elections
   D. it is controlled by a political framework

Answer: D

Explanation: Both private and public sectors may have various tax arrangements. Public and private sectors equally may offer public services, and be influenced by elections. Only the public sector is controlled by specific political criteria framework.

QUESTION 20

What is the length of a term for a United States Senator?

   A. 2 years
   B. 4 years
   C. 6 years
   D. 8 years

Answer: C

Explanation: A United States Senator can only hold a 6 years term.

QUESTION 21

When national output rises, the economy is said to be in

    A. an inflation
    B. an expansion
    C. a deflation
    D. a recession

Answer: B

Explanation: An economic expansion is an increase in the level of economic activity (national output rises) and of the goods and services available.

QUESTION 22

Which of the following beliefs did the Ancient Greeks and the modern United States share?

    A. laws are critical to ensure societies remain stable
    B. leaders should be chosen by political parties
    C. buildings should not have columns
    D. certain groups should not vote

Answer: A

Explanation: Both Ancient Greek and the modern United States were aligned with the fact that laws are important.

QUESTION 23

Column A lists theoretical models of economic organizations and Column B lists their major strength. Which of the following is the best match?

Letter	Column A	Column B
A	Command	is less likely than other economic systems to have problems related to scarcity
B	Mixed	combines the economic productivity of a market system with the distributional efficiency of a command system
C	Traditional	is more likely than other economic systems to use democratic procedures to make basic economic decisions
D	Market	provides a strong basis for the expression of state-based initiatives

Answer: A

Explanation: Command economy is one that is less likely than other economic systems to have problems related to scarcity.

QUESTION 24

Which of the following best describes how the United States' democracy differs from democracy in Athens, Greece?

    A. Individuals in United States democracy vote depending on race.
    B. Democracy in the United States is only used during election season.
    C. People in the United States directly vote on which laws are implemented.
    D. The United States elects representatives as oppose to voting on laws directly.

Answer: D

Explanation: Americans vote political leaders to represent them in the Senate and House. The leaders are individuals voting on the laws. Americans are not directly involved in voting for laws.

QUESTION 25

Which of the following significantly contributed to the fall of the Roman Empire?

    A. individuals' refusal to participate in the democratic process
    B. a period of excessive disorder and a weak national government
    C. growth of surrounding countries
    D. excessive national debt

Answer: B

Explanation: There was a period of excessive disorder and a weak national government, and a lack of establishment of feudalism that resulted in the fall of the Roman Empire.

QUESTION 26

In World War II, which two cities were destroyed by atomic bombs before Japan agreed to surrender?

    A. Tokyo and Hiroshima
    B. Nagasaki and Shanghai
    C. Hiroshima and Nagasaki
    D. Nagasaki and Tokyo

Answer: C

Explanation: Hiroshima and Nagasaki were the two cities destroyed by atomic bombs before Japan agreed to surrender.

QUESTION 27

What was a major effect of World War II on women and minorities in the United States?

    A. increased opportunities in the workplace
    B. equal pay for equal work for all individuals
    C. increased participation in democratic process
    D. selective service requirements extended to women and minorities

Answer: A

Explanation: The war resulted in a need of many army soldiers, rangers, marines, paratroopers, sailors, pilots, nurses, and industrial workers. As a result, a lot of jobs were left behind, which increased opportunities in the workplace for women and minorities.

QUESTION 28

     I.   lithosphere --- landforms
     II.   hydrosphere ---water features
     III.   biosphere --- nature

Of the above, which of the following is/are correctly matched?
    A. I only
    B. II only
    C. I and II
    D. I, II, and III

Answer: D

Explanation: The lithosphere is the solid Earth—landforms, rocks, soils, etc. The hydrosphere includes the waters of the Earth such as oceans, rivers, etc. The biosphere is composed of all living things.

QUESTION 29

The United States Constitution guarantees the right to a writ of habeas corpus. The main reason for this was to

    A. to prevent the illegal imprisonment of individual in the United States.
    B. to prevent illegal arrests.
    C. to prevent search of homes without warrants.
    D. to give individuals the right to a speedy trail.

Answer: A

Explanation: A writ of habeas corpus means to produce a body. It is a court order to a person holding someone in custody to bring the imprisoned individual to the court issuing the order.

QUESTION 30

     I.   Bill of Rights
     II.   Articles of Confederation
     III.   Declaration of Independence
     IV.   United States Constitution

Which of the following correctly orders the above documents starting from the first written?

    A. II, I, III, IV
    B. III, II, IV, I
    C. III, II, I, IV
    D. I, II, IV, III

Answer: B

Explanation: Declaration of Independence came in 1776. Articles of Confederation came in 1781. The United States Constitution was ratified in 1788. Bill of Rights was ratified in 1791.

QUESTION 31

Draining of the Everglades has been done primarily for:

    A. urban development
    B. economic development
    C. government development
    D. social development

Answer: A

Explanation: The draining of the Everglades has been done primarily for agricultural and urban development.

QUESTION 32

Individuals who lead and supported the Chinese Revolution of 1949 broke mainly with the Chinese past in their:

- A. creation of a Paleolithic, centralized state
- B. culture of remaining isolated
- C. stress on class conflict, science, and materialism
- D. ability to increase exports

Answer: C

Explanation: Chinese Revolution of 1949 broke most determinedly with the Chinese past in their stress on class conflict, science, and materialism.

QUESTION 33

The State of Rhode Island can be best used for measuring which of the following?

- A.   City of St. Petersburg, Florida
- B.   State of Texas
- C.   State of Delaware
- D.   City of Indianapolis, Indiana

Answer: B

Explanation: Rhode Island is the smallest State. Rhode Island can be used to measure another State. Delaware is not the best to measure using Rhode Island as a reference because Delaware's size is just as small as Rhode Island. City of St. Petersburg, Florida and City of Indianapolis, Indiana are too small to measure using Rhode Island as a reference. The State of Texas is big enough to measure using Rhode Island as a reference.

QUESTION 34

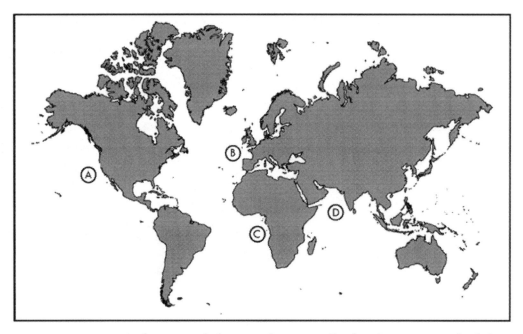

Merchants use monsoon winds to travel along trade routes. In the above map, which location did merchants historically use?

A. A
B. B
C. C
D. D

Answer: D

Explanation: Letter D is the Indian Ocean, which has been used by merchants for monsoon winds to travel along trade routes.

QUESTION 35

The United States government and the state governments share responsibilities of _____.

    A. declaring schools unfit
    B. operating post offices
    C. conducting elections
    D. establishing courts

Answer: D

Explanation: The United States government and the state governments share responsibilities of establishing courts.

QUESTION 36

The following are groups within a local police department:

    I.   street patrol
    II.   detective work
    III.   domestic cases
    IV.   traffic control

The organizational structure is a reflection of which economic concept:

    A. division of labor
    B. opportunity cost
    C. organization
    D. economic efficiency

Answer: A

Explanation: Division of Labor is the separation of tasks in any economic system so that individuals may specialize and effectively contribute to society. The local police department has these positions were individuals are trained to carryout specialized duties.

QUESTION 37

Which of the following was the main reason for replacing the Articles of Confederation with the United States Constitution?

    A. limited the power of the national government
    B. expand the powers of the national government
    C. decreased the autonomy of state and local government
    D. made the government more accountable for the people

Answer: B

Explanation: The Articles of Confederation outlined a weak national government. Leaders, such as George Washington and Alexander Hamilton, saw a need for a stronger national government, prompting the development of the United States Constitution.

QUESTION 38

A circular model shows what feature of a market economy?

    A. exchange of goods and services
    B. exchange of hazards
    C. global model
    D. no opportunity cost involved

Answer: A

Explanation: A circular model describes the flow of money and products throughout the economy in a very simplified way.

QUESTION 39

In the latter part of the nineteenth century, the United States agricultural business in the Midwest started to transform from a market system of small family farms to one dominated by large commercialized farms. This change is mostly due to:

A. the increasing population density in the region
B. the technological advances in railroad transportation
C. the posts Cold War impact
D. the increase in exports of agricultural resources

Answer: B

Explanation: Advances in technology allowed individuals to better the agricultural processes, increasing business. Advances in technology resulted in the railroad transportation system allowing businesses to reach additional customers. With increased demand, the need for advance commercialized farms increased.

QUESTION 40

To better understand the impact of ancient Greece on the historical development of Western civilization, the best resources to examine are related to:

A. increase of absolute monarchies
B. causes of the Reformation
C. emergence of feudalism
D. origins of the Renaissance

Answer: D

Explanation: Ancient Greece is well known for the Renaissance, so reviewing the origins of the Renaissance will provide a good understanding of the impact.

QUESTION 41

In the United States, local governments normally use a significant amount of their resources to:

    A. give mental health services
    B. impose environmental regulations
    C. provide elementary and secondary schools programs
    D. develop outside art structures

Answer: C

Explanation: Environmental regulations are regulated at the federal level. Art projects will not cost as much as school programs. Individuals with mental health issues are far less than those individuals attending elementary and secondary schools. Local governments normally use a significant amount of their resources to provide programs for elementary and secondary schools.

QUESTION 42

A topographic map is best used for:

    A. determining the difference in elevation between a river and a close by mountain range
    B. knowing the types of coastal landforms found in a region
    C. locating the shortest route between two places
    D. comparing the population distribution of two states

Answer: A

Explanation: A topographic map is best used for determining the difference in elevation between a river and a close by mountain range.

QUESTION 43

_____ is the process by which a person or group language/culture comes to resemble those of another group.

    A. assimilation
    B. diffusion
    C. syncretism
    D. resemblance

Answer: A

Explanation: Assimilation is the process by which a person or group language/culture comes to resemble those of another group.

QUESTION 44

Which of the following is best related to the principle of popular sovereignty guaranteed by the U.S. Constitution?

    A. "All courts shall be open, and every person, for an injury done to him in his person, property or reputation, shall have remedy by due course of law."
    B. "Every citizen may freely speak, write and publish his sentiments on all subjects, being responsible for the abuse of that liberty."
    C. "The people shall be secure in their persons, houses, papers and possessions from unreasonable searches or seizures."
    D. "All political power is inherent in the people . . . and they have at all times an undeniable and indefeasible right to alter their form of government in such manner as they may think expedient."

Answer: D

Explanation: Popular sovereignty is the principle that the authority of a state and its government is created and sustained by the agreement of its people. The quote that represents principle of popular sovereignty is Option D.

QUESTION 45

Which of the following was a major impact of World War I?

    A. the onset of economic depression in America
    B. the rise of nationalist movements in the Austro-Hungarian empire
    C. the rise of communism in Russia
    D. the limited number of jobs in America

Answer: A

Explanation: One major cause of World War I was the onset of the economic depression in America. This slowly led America into the Great Depression.

QUESTION 46

Under international law, which of the following is a violation of human rights?

    A. a prisoner arrested is not allowed to communicate with family members
    B. a refugee is unable to obtain work in the host country
    C. a teenager is not allowed to travel to his parents' home country
    D. an individual arrested without being given his/her Miranda rights

Answer: A

Explanation: Under international law, a prisoner arrested is not allowed to communicate with family members is a violation of human rights. International human rights laws are in place to protect human rights at the international, regional, and domestic levels.

QUESTION 47

Which of the following is a difference in the way a democratic and authoritarian government operates?

    A. the selection of government leaders
    B. having a governing document
    C. the currency system
    D. the enforcement of law

Answer: A

Explanation: The authoritarian government has the power, and in a democracy, the people have the power. Democratic system allows individuals to select their leaders. Option B is not the answer as both governments will have a governing document.

QUESTION 48

Which of the following provides the basic reason for the support of public education in the United States?

    A. skilled labor
    B. trained professors
    C. informed citizens
    D. educated leaders

Answer: C

Explanation: Informed citizens are critical for the continued development and advancement of society. Informed citizens also make sound decisions during elections.

QUESTION 49

The Napoleonic Code was a

    A. military strategy
    B. legal system
    C. political system
    D. behavioral system

Answer: B

Explanation: The Napoleonic Code was a legal framework for France.

QUESTION 50

Which of the following is an inaccurate statement?

    A. all taxes and other revenues exceed government expenditures for a year is called a budget surplus
    B. revenues and expenditures are equal during a given period is called a balanced budget
    C. expenditures exceed revenue from taxes is called a cyclical crisis.
    D. actual dollar expenditures, revenues, and deficits in a given period is called an actual budget

Answer: C

Explanation: Difference between the actual budget and the structural budget is called a cyclical budget. Expenditures exceed revenue from taxes is called a budget deficit.

QUESTION 51

Zora Neale Hurston and Langston Hughes were a part of what period in American history?

    A. Harlem Renaissance
    B. Restoration Age
    C. Old English
    D. Victorian literature

Answer: A

Explanation: Zora Neale Hurston and Langston Hughes were involved in the Harlem Renaissance period.

QUESTION 52

A change from a direct democracy to a representative democracy is best undertaken when

    A. economic status of people change for the better.
    B. nations acquire additional land.
    C. population increases.
    D. many individuals are not voting.

Answer: C

Explanation: When the population is less, individuals can be directly involved in democracy. When the population increases, there is a need for a representative to represent groups to be able to have a smooth, organized democratic process.

QUESTION 53

After World War II, the United States had a program that provided money, supplies, and machinery to assist European counties in rebuilding. What was the program called?

    A. Marshall Plan
    B. Four Point Program
    C. Truman Doctrine
    D. New Deal

Answer: A

Explanation: The Marshall Plan was a United States program to support Western Europe in rebuilding Western European economies after the end of World War II.

QUESTION 54

Which of the following is most critical for a historical researcher to consider when reading through resources on individuals being interviewed on the impact of the Great Depression had on the State in 1970?

    A. individuals say what they think the interviewer wants to hear
    B. individuals don't understand the impact it had on history
    C. individuals minds have changed over the years
    D. individuals location at the time

Answer: B

Explanation: These individuals mentioned in the question lived through the Great Depression, so they do not know the impact of the Great Depression decades later.

QUESTION 55

Population and Square Miles of Countries

Country	Land in square miles	Population in millions
Israel	7550	5.4
Iraq	168860	19.2
Jordan	34340	3.6
Kuwait	7102	1.7

According to the above data, which country is the most densely populated?

A. Iraq113
B. Jordan 104
C. Israel 715
D. Kuwait 239

Answer: C

Explanation: Population Density = Number of People / Land Area. Using this formula, the population density of Israel is about 715 people/miles. Another way to complete this question is round all the numbers and then divide. From there, population density of Israel is shown to be the mostly dense.

This page is intentionally left blank.

Practice Test 2

This page is intentionally left blank.

Exam Answer Sheet Test 2

Below is an optional answer sheet to use to document answers.

Question Number	Selected Answer	Question Number	Selected Answer
1		29	
2		30	
3		31	
4		32	
5		33	
6		34	
7		35	
8		36	
9		37	
10		38	
11		39	
12		40	
13		41	
14		42	
15		43	
16		44	
17		45	
18		46	
19		47	
20		48	
21		49	
22		50	
23		51	
24		52	
25		53	
26		54	
27		55	
28			

This page is intentionally left blank.

QUESTION 1

Investment bankers are most likely to support legislation that will

    A. increase exports to the United States
    B. reduce the scope of antitrust laws
    C. involve government agencies in approval processes
    D. decrease imports to the United States

Answer:

QUESTION 2

What would happen to supply and demand if a large number of orange trees were to get a infected with a disease?

    A. supply increase and demand increase
    B. supply decrease and demand decrease
    C. supply decrease and demand increase
    D. supply decrease and demand remains the same

Answer:

QUESTION 3

Which of the following was a significant consequence of the Irish Potato Famine that occurred from 1845 to 1849?

    A. the increase in population in Ireland
    B. the emigration of approximately 1.5 million individuals to North America
    C. the increase regulation on distribution of potatoes
    D. the overthrow of the authority in Ireland

Answer:

QUESTION 4

  I. Great Pyramid of Giza
  II. Temple of Artemis of Babylon
  III. Colossus of Rhodes

Of the above, which of the following is/are part of the Seven Wonders of the Ancient World?

  A. I only
  B. II only
  C. I and II
  D. I, II, and III

Answer:

QUESTION 5

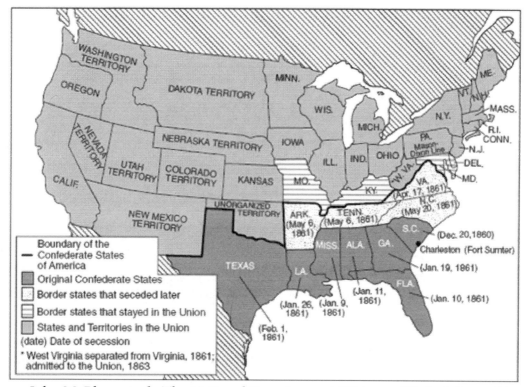

Source: John M. Blum et. al., The National Experience: A History of United States. Harcourt Brace Jovanovich, 1981 (adapted)

What is the most accurate title for this map shown above?

    A. Closing the Frontier

    B. A Nation Divided

    C. Results of Reconstruction

    D. Compromise of 1850

Answer:

QUESTION 6

Immigrates coming to the United States

Year	Total Number of Immigrants
1920	430,230
1925	295,644
1930	245,644
1935	35,329
1940	70,328
1945	39,193
1950	248,932

Which of the following is accurately supported by the information presented in the table above?

A. The United States passed immigration laws that limited the number of individuals entering the country in the 1920s.
B. The United States saw increase population from Mexico in 1950.
C. The United States halted immigration in the years after World War I.
D. The United States saw a reduction in jobs after 1920, so the country limited number of individuals entering the country in the 1930s.

Answer:

QUESTION 7

I.   paying taxes
II.   voting
III. registering for the selective service

Which of the following is/are responsibilities of all adult citizens?

A. I only
B. II only
C. I and II
D. II and III

Answer:

QUESTION 8

In regards to the United States invading Iraq in 2003, which of the following issues led some Americans to lose support for the invasion over time?

    A. the increase number of troops going to Iraq
    B. the lack of evidence for weapons of mass destruction in Iraq
    C. the increasing cost of war
    D. the inability of United States to rebuild Iraq

Answer:

QUESTION 9

Which of the following is the main purpose for the creation of the North Atlantic Treaty Organization founded in 1949?

    A. encourage open trade with North American states
    B. keep the Soviet Union from taking over western Europe
    C. keep a united front against world terrorism
    D. encourage alliance to ensure economic growth around the world

Answer:

QUESTION 10

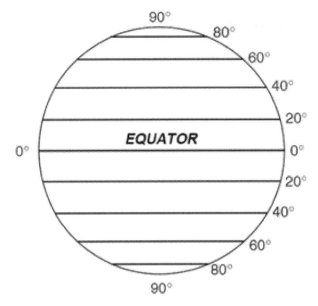

What is depicted in the above image?

    A. lines of latitude
    B. lines of distance
    C. lines of longitude
    D. lines of equator

Answer:

QUESTION 11

What does the Declaration of Independence declare as a significant right of the people, when a government is unsuccessful in protecting their freedoms?

    A. dispose the government
    B. support the government
    C. hold town hall meetings
    D. impeach the President

Answer:

QUESTION 12

Under the Constitution, what is one way that a branch of government checks another branch?

    A. Courts can decide the constitutionality of laws made by Congress.
    B. Congress writes the laws, but the president passes them into law.
    C. The president commands the army and can declare war.
    D. The president decides the tax amount, and Congress collects the tax.

Answer:

QUESTION 13

Which of the following best describes federalism?

    A. states and a central government share power
    B. states have more control in local issues
    C. central government has no power over the states
    D. central government has all the power over the states

Answer:

QUESTION 14

What was the main reason for imposing a tax on whiskey?

    A. to minimize drinking
    B. to pay off the national debt
    C. to supporting amendment to ban whiskey
    D. to increase funds to support the military

Answer:

QUESTION 15

Which of the following best indicates the colonists' most effective way to resist British taxes prior to the American Revolution?

A. overthrowing the government
B. not buying specific goods
C. voicing opinions to speak to Parliament
D. establishing legislation

Answer:

QUESTION 16

I. Thought that the Parliament was giving an unfair position to British merchants.
II. Thought that they had not been fairly represented in the decision regarding taxes made by Parliament.
III. Thought that they could control all of the merchandise that was being imported and exported out of the Port of Boston.

Which of the following accurately states Boston colonists' reason to destroying the tea cargo?

A. I only
B. I and II
C. I and III
D. II and III

Answer:

QUESTION 17

Which of the following is an effect of the Columbian Exchange?

    A. The exchange of animals and food had a significant impact on later societies.
    B. The spread of diseases increased and reduced the population worldwide.
    C. Triangular trade profits remained stable.
    D. There was an increase in jobs in America.

Answer:

QUESTION 18

Democratic societies have written constitutions for the main purpose of:

    A. holding those who govern responsible to the governed
    B. protecting the social rights of individuals
    C. establishing laws that protect Americans
    D. ensuring a free economy

Answer:

QUESTION 19

Which of the following ideas are contained in the Declaration of Independence?

    A. the right to vote for all individuals
    B. the colonists' complaints against the king
    C. the declaration of freedom from slavery
    D. the outline of a new American government

Answer:

QUESTION 20

Which of the following descriptions is inaccurate?

A	Samuel Adams	Leader of the pro-independence movement Signer of the Declaration of Independence Founder of the Committees of Correspondence
B	Thomas Paine	Wrote Common Sense to advocate for independence from Great Britain Wrote The Crisis to encourage Americans to not give up and to keep fighting for independence
C	Benjamin Franklin	Helped write the Declaration of Independence Signer of the Declaration of Independence Ambassador to France
D	Thomas Jefferson	Delegate to the Continental Congress, Author of the Constitution Governor of Georgia

Answer:

QUESTION 21

Which of the following issues did not result in a major compromise at the first Constitutional Convention?

 A. determining state representation in Congress
 B. separating the powers of the central government
 C. determining trade authority for Congress to regulate
 D. allowing slaves to be counted in state's population

Answer:

QUESTION 22

The Great Compromise, the Three-fifths Compromise, and the Commerce and Slave Trade Compromise were all compromises at the _____.

 A. signing of the Constitution
 B. Constitutional Convention of 1787
 C. Constitutional Convention of 1836
 D. signing of the Bill of Rights

Answer:

QUESTION 23

 I.   Federalists founded by Alexander Hamilton and John Adams
 II.   Democratic Republicans founded by Andrew Jackson and Martin Van Buren.
 III.   National Republicans founded by John Quincy Adams and Henry Clay.

Of the above, which of the following is an inaccurate statement?

 A. I only
 B. II only
 C. I and II
 D. I and III

Answer:

QUESTION 24

What power is only exclusive to the Legislative Branch?

    A. impeachment power
    B. implement laws
    C. declare war
    D. interpret the law

Answer:

QUESTION 25

Which of the following is the main purpose of the Lewis and Clark expedition?

    A. find land to eventually find gold
    B. find a waterway from the US to the Pacific Ocean
    C. find land to establish settlement
    D. find a route for the Native Americans

Answer:

QUESTION 26

How did the Louisiana Territory of the Louisiana Purchase protect the nation's trade?

    A. The United States controlled all trade coming in and out of the Port of New Orleans.
    B. It kept the port out of the hands of foreign power.
    C. The United States could cut off access to the port any time.
    D. All of the above

Answer:

QUESTION 27

Which of the following United States government policies was a direct consequence of the Trail of Tears of 1838?

    A. taking Native American lands east of the Mississippi River
    B. adding taxes to Native American lands east of the Mississippi River
    C. stopping Native Americans from gaining lands with value
    D. restricting Native Americans from moving

Answer:

QUESTION 28

Women's work both inside and outside the home was impacted the most by which of the following technological advances of the Industrial Revolution?

    A. the mechanization of weaving and spinning
    B. the invention of the phone
    C. the invention of the steam engine
    D. the invention of the sewing machine

Answer:

QUESTION 29

Which of the following was Jackson's solution to white settlers' hunger for land?

    A. Northwest Ordinance
    B. Indian Removal Act
    C. Land Removal Act
    D. Westward Expansion Act

Answer:

QUESTION 30

Which of the following is inaccurate regarding the Bill of Rights?

    A. The amendments were written part of the original Constitution.
    B. The amendments give rights such as freedom of speech and religion.
    C. Many states refused to accept the Constitution without the Bill of Rights.
    D. The Bill of Rights is an evergreen aspect of the Constitution.

Answer:

QUESTION 31

Which of the following indicates that the government may do only those things that the people have given it the power to do so?

    A. limited government
    B. checks and balances
    C. popular sovereignty
    D. separation of power

Answer:

QUESTION 32

Which of the following amendments gave women the right to vote?

    A. 13th amendment
    B. 15th amendment
    C. 16th amendment
    D. 19th amendment

Answer:

QUESTION 33

Which of the following best describes a major effect of Neolithic agricultural revolution?

    A. additional religious groups forming
    B. the establishing of permanent settlements
    C. equal distribution of wealth
    D. additional military resources

Answer:

QUESTION 34

    I.   Pakistan
    II.   Bangladesh
    III.   Malaysia
    IV.   Singapore

When India split into three parts what were the names of the other two parts?

A. I and II
B. I and III
C. II and III
D. II and IV

Answer:

QUESTION 35

Which of the following events did not contribute to Cold War tensions?

A. United States support to provide food to the citizens of Berlin
B. the establishment of the North Atlantic Treaty Organization
C. rejection of the Treaty of Versailles by the Senate
D. significant economic support for western Europe due to the Marshall Plan.

Answer:

QUESTION 36

What case did Brown v. Board of Education overturn the ruling of?

A. Dredd Scott
B. United States v. Lopez
C. Plessy v. Ferguson
D. West Virginia State Board of Education v. Barnette

Answer:

QUESTION 37

Which Constitutional amendment was intended to protect the rights of the newly freed slaves?

    A. 13th Amendment
    B. 14th Amendment
    C. 15th Amendment
    D. 16th Amendment

Answer:

QUESTION 38

During the Reconstruction Period, literacy tests and poll taxes were used primarily due to the implementation of which of the following amendments?

    A. 13th Amendment
    B. 14th Amendment
    C. 15th Amendment
    D. 16th Amendment

Answer:

QUESTION 39

Which of the following civilization was first associated with the concept of democracy?

    A. Greeks
    B. Incans
    C. Egyptians
    D. Romans

Answer:

QUESTION 40

Of the following, which best describes the preamble of the United States Constitution?

    A. purpose of government
    B. summary of the Constitution
    C. limitation of government
    D. distribution of power

Answer:

QUESTION 41

Of the following, who is considered the principal author of the United States Constitution?

    A. Thomas Jefferson
    B. James Madison
    C. John Adams
    D. George Washington

Answer:

QUESTION 42

How is a political map different than a physical map?

    A. They are exactly the same.
    B. One is a globe while the other is actually a map.
    C. A political map always pretends to be 3D whereas a physical map never pretends to be 3D.
    D. A political map focuses on boundaries and a physical map focuses the geography of the area

Answer:

QUESTION 43

According to the idea of supply and demand, a decrease in production rates of oil will mostly likely result in _____.

    A. increase in oil prices for consumers
    B. increase in stock prices
    C. increase in wages
    D. increase in capital investment

Answer:

QUESTION 44

Which of the following is the best tool for teaching students the geographic concept of hemispheres?

    A. two-dimensional maps
    B. three-dimensional maps
    C. geography textbook
    D. positioning machine

Answer:

QUESTION 45

Which of the following countries is least self-sufficient in regards to natural resources needed for modern industry?

    A. United Kingdom
    B. France
    C. Japan
    D. United States

Answer:

QUESTION 46

High population density along coastlines and early settlement best contributed to which of the following?

    A. larger habitat for animals
    B. access to trade routes
    C. increase communication
    D. increase building construction

Answer:

QUESTION 47

A company is introducing a new product line globally. The information initially travels through a process known as:

    A. culture diffusion
    B. contagious diffusion
    C. hierarchical diffusion
    D. movement diffusion

Answer:

QUESTION 48

Which of the following religions did not originate in eastern Mediterranean?

    A. Judaism
    B. Christianity
    C. Islam
    D. Buddhism

Answer:

QUESTION 49

How do earthquakes create mountain ranges?

    A. collision of continental plates at fault zones
    B. erosion of the earth
    C. distribution of forces during earthquakes
    D. the range difference in elevation

Answer:

QUESTION 50

Which of the following is a major sociological difference between postindustrial and preindustrial societies?

    A. people are less likely to discuss religion in preindustrial society
    B. people are more focused on oneself than others in preindustrial society
    C. social status is likely to be decided by nonmonetary standards in preindustrial society
    D. women were more involved in business discussions in preindustrial society

Answer:

QUESTION 51

Which of the following would be considered a primary source for a research project about World War II?

    A. an encyclopedia article
    B. a letter written by a soldier to his brother during the war
    C. a biography of a prominent Union general during the war
    D. a novel set in northern Virginia that takes place during the war

Answer:

QUESTION 52

While conducting research on United States politics of the late nineteenth century, a historian considers consulting the autobiography of a prominent politician who was alive in the late nineteenth century. Doing so is most likely to help the historian

    A. to evaluate the long-term consequences of decisions made in the late nineteenth century.
    B. to determine the exact sequence of events.
    C. to obtain insight into contemporary values and beliefs.
    D. to give perspective of individuals' feeling in the late nineteenth century.

Answer:

QUESTION 53

The Federalist Paper is historically most relevant for which of the following?

    A. foundation for writing the Constitution
    B. foundation for the Bill of Rights
    C. foundation of the analysis and explanation of the Constitution
    D. foundation for the Declaration of Independence

Answer:

QUESTION 54

Which of the following is the best reason for why few bills become laws?

    A. the bill is written poorly
    B. the process is too long
    C. there are many opportunities to terminate a bill
    D. president has the power to veto

Answer:

QUESTION 55

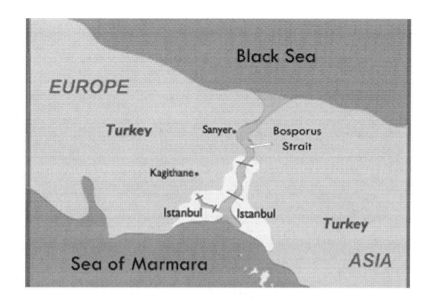

Istanbul's relative location, which is shown on the maps, contributes to controlling which of the following?

    A. river
    B. ocean
    C. strait
    D. marsh area

Answer:

This page is intentionally left blank.

Answer Key Test 2

Question Number	Correct Answer	Question Number	Correct Answer
1	B	29	B
2	B	30	A
3	B	31	A
4	D	32	D
5	B	33	B
6	A	34	A
7	B	35	C
8	B	36	C
9	B	37	B
10	A	38	A
11	A	39	A
12	A	40	C
13	A	41	B
14	B	42	D
15	B	43	A
16	B	44	B
17	A	45	C
18	A	46	B
19	B	47	C
20	D	48	D
21	B	49	A
22	B	50	C
23	B	51	B
24	A	52	C
25	B	53	A
26	D	54	C
27	A	55	C
28	A		

NOTE: Getting approximately 80% of the questions correct increases chances of obtaining passing score on the real exam. This varies from different states and university programs.

This page is intentionally left blank.

Elementary Education – Social Studies – Questions and Answers – Test 2
55 Questions

QUESTION 1

Investment bankers are most likely to support legislation that will

A. increase exports to the United States
B. reduce the scope of antitrust laws
C. involve government agencies in approval processes
D. decrease imports to the United States

Answer: B

Explanation: Investment bankers work in the financial institution, and they primary do business to increase capital for various entities. Investor bankers prefer to not have laws that will prevent them or slow them in doing their job. They will support legislation that reduces antitrust laws.

QUESTION 2

What would happen to supply and demand if a large number of orange trees were to get a infected with a disease?

A. supply increase and demand increase
B. supply decrease and demand decrease
C. supply decrease and demand increase
D. supply decrease and demand remains the same

Answer: B

Explanation: There will be fewer oranges as the trees are infected with a disease, so supply will decrease. Because there is a disease linked to some orange trees, most individuals will not want to buy oranges; the demand will decrease.

QUESTION 3

Which of the following was a significant consequence of the Irish Potato Famine that occurred from 1845 to 1849?

    A. the increase in population in Ireland
    B. the emigration of approximately 1.5 million individuals to North America
    C. the increase regulation on distribution of potatoes
    D. the overthrow of the authority in Ireland

Answer: B

Explanation: The Famine years of 1845 to 1849 resulted in many individuals to move to different countries. Approximately 1.5 million individuals moved to North America.

QUESTION 4

    I.   Great Pyramid of Giza
    II.   Temple of Artemis of Babylon
    III.   Colossus of Rhodes

Of the above, which of the following is/are part of the Seven Wonders of the Ancient World?

    A. I only
    B. II only
    C. I and II
    D. I, II, and III

Answer: D

Explanation: The Seven Wonders of the Ancient World were:

- the Great Pyramid at Giza, Egypt.
- the Hanging Gardens of Babylon.
- the Statue of Zeus at Olympia, Greece.
- the Temple of Artemis at Ephesus.
- the Mausoleum at Halicarnassus.
- the Colossus of Rhodes.
- the Lighthouse at Alexandria, Egypt.

QUESTION 5

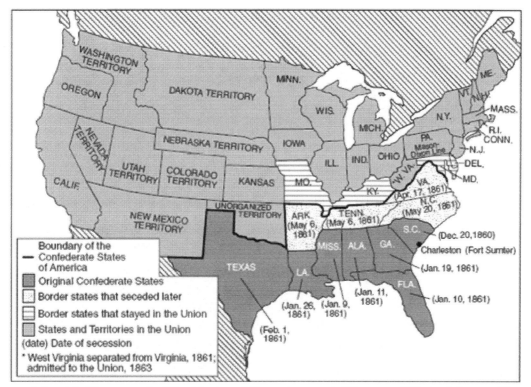

Source: John M. Blum et. al., The National Experience: A History of United States. Harcourt Brace Jovanovich, 1981 (adapted)

What is the most accurate title for this map shown above?

A. Closing the Frontier
B. A Nation Divided
C. Results of Reconstruction
D. Compromise of 1850

Answer: B

Explanation: The map shows the boundary of the Confederate States of America, so the best title is "A Nation Divided".

QUESTION 6

Immigrates coming to the United States

Year	Total Number of Immigrants
1920	430,230
1925	295,644
1930	245,644
1935	35,329
1940	70,328
1945	39,193
1950	248,932

Which of the following is accurately supported by the information presented in the table above?

    A. The United States passed immigration laws that limited the number of individuals entering the country in the 1920s.
    B. The United States saw increase population from Mexico in 1950.
    C. The United States halted immigration in the years after World War I.
    D. The United States saw a reduction in jobs after 1920, so the country limited number of individuals entering the country in the 1930s.

Answer: A

Explanation: The only option that makes sense and is supported by the data is option A. In 1920, the total number immigrants were 430,230. After that, there was a decline in immigrants, which indicates the United States passed migration laws that limited the number of individuals entering the country.

QUESTION 7

     I.   paying taxes
     II.   voting
     III.   registering for the selective service

Which of the following is/are responsibilities of all adult citizens?

    A. I only
    B. II only
    C. I and II
    D. II and III

Answer: B

Explanation: All adult citizens have the responsibility to vote, regardless of whether or not they. Paying taxes is also mandatory for all individuals residing in America. However, some individuals may not be working, which eliminates paying taxes as a correct option.

QUESTION 8

In regards to the United States invading Iraq in 2003, which of the following issues led some Americans to lose support for the invasion over time?

    A. the increase number of troops going to Iraq
    B. the lack of evidence for weapons of mass destruction in Iraq
    C. the increasing cost of war
    D. the inability of United States to rebuild Iraq

Answer: B

Explanation: The American government could not produce solid evidence that weapons of mass destruction existed in Iraq. Without this evidence, Americans began to lose support for the invasion over time.

QUESTION 9

Which of the following is the main purpose for the creation of the North Atlantic Treaty Organization founded in 1949?

    A. encourage open trade with North American states
    B. keep the Soviet Union from taking over western Europe
    C. keep a united front against world terrorism
    D. encourage alliance to ensure economic growth around the world

Answer: B

Explanation: The North Atlantic Treaty Organization was to unify and strengthen the Western Allies' military response to keep the Soviet Union from taking over Western Europe.

QUESTION 10

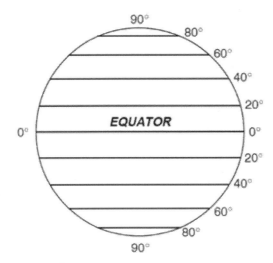

What is depicted in the above image?

    A. lines of latitude
    B. lines of distance
    C. lines of longitude
    D. lines of equator

Answer: A

Explanation: Lines of latitude, or parallels, run east–west parallel to the equator.

QUESTION 11

What does the Declaration of Independence declare as a significant right of the people, when a government is unsuccessful in protecting their freedoms?

A. dispose the government
B. support the government
C. hold town hall meetings
D. impeach the President

Answer: A

Explanation: The Declaration of Independence gives individuals the right to dispose the government, if the government is unsuccessful in protecting their freedoms. Option B makes no sense; there is no need to support the government if it is not doing its job. A document like the Declaration of Independence is not going to have indication of holding town hall meetings, so Option C is eliminated. Individuals do not have the right to impeach the President, so Option D is eliminated.

QUESTION 12

Under the Constitution, what is one way that a branch of government checks another branch?

A. Courts can decide the constitutionality of laws made by Congress.
B. Congress writes the laws, but the president passes them into law.
C. The president commands the army and can declare war.
D. The president decides the tax amount, and Congress collects the tax.

Answer: A

Explanation: Checks and balances allows each branch of the government (executive, judicial, and legislative) to have some measure of influence over the other branches, such as blocking procedures of the other branches. Option A is an example of a branch of government checking another branch.

QUESTION 13

Which of the following best describes federalism?

    A. states and a central government share power
    B. states have more control in local issues
    C. central government has no power over the states
    D. central government has all the power over the states

Answer: A

Explanation: Federalism is a system of government in which entities such as states share power with a central government.

QUESTION 14

What was the main reason for imposing a tax on whiskey?

    A. to minimize drinking
    B. to pay off the national debt
    C. to supporting amendment to ban whiskey
    D. to increase funds to support the military

Answer: B

Explanation: In 1791, the "whiskey tax" was the first tax imposed on a domestic product by the newly formed federal government. This was done to generate revenue to help reduce the national debt.

QUESTION 15

Which of the following best indicates the colonists' most effective way to resist British taxes prior to the American Revolution?

    A. overthrowing the government
    B. not buying specific goods
    C. voicing opinions to speak to Parliament
    D. establishing legislation

Answer: B

Explanation: Colonist did not overthrow the government, and the colonist did not have the authority to establish legislation. At the time, voicing opinion to speak to Parliament was not the most effective way or even possible most times. The colonists can refuse to buy specific goods to resist British taxes.

QUESTION 16

    I.   Thought that the Parliament was giving an unfair position to British merchants.
    II.   Thought that they had not been fairly represented in the decision regarding taxes made by Parliament.
    III.   Thought that they could control all of the merchandise that was being imported and exported out of the Port of Boston.

Which of the following accurately states Boston colonists' reason to destroying the tea cargo?

    A. I only
    B. I and II
    C. I and III
    D. II and III

Answer: B

Explanation: Boston colonists believed Parliament was giving an unfair advantage to British merchants, and Boston colonists felt that they had not been represented in the decisions about taxes made by Parliament this prompted them to destroy the tea cargo.

QUESTION 17

Which of the following is an effect of the Columbian Exchange?

    A. The exchange of animals and food had a significant impact on later societies.
    B. The spread of diseases increased and reduced the population worldwide.
    C. Triangular trade profits remained stable.
    D. There was an increase in jobs in America.

Answer: A

Explanation: Over time, crops native to the Americas, such as corn, became typical food in the diets of people in Europe and many parts of the world. With these foods, individuals lived longer as substantial nutrition was provided. There was diseases being spread mainly between Europe and America, but not necessary the entire world; eliminating choice B.

QUESTION 18

Democratic societies have written constitutions for the main purpose of:

    A. holding those who govern responsible to the governed
    B. protecting the social rights of individuals
    C. establishing laws that protect Americans
    D. ensuring a free economy

Answer: A

Explanation: Constitutions give those who are elected to office the guidelines and authority to govern. Individuals who are elected to government offices must follow laws within written constitutions to ensure they are being held responsible and accountable to those who elected them into office.

QUESTION 19

Which of the following ideas are contained in the Declaration of Independence?

    A. the right to vote for all individuals
    B. the colonists' complaints against the king
    C. the declaration of freedom from slavery
    D. the outline of a new American government

Answer: B

Explanation: The main purpose of the Declaration of Independence was to outline the complaints the colonists had against the king.

QUESTION 20

Which of the following descriptions is inaccurate?

A	Samuel Adams	Leader of the pro-independence movement Signer of the Declaration of Independence Founder of the Committees of Correspondence
B	Thomas Paine	Wrote Common Sense to advocate for independence from Great Britain Wrote The Crisis to encourage Americans to not give up and to keep fighting for independence
C	Benjamin Franklin	Helped write the Declaration of Independence Signer of the Declaration of Independence Ambassador to France
D	Thomas Jefferson	Delegate to the Continental Congress, Author of the Constitution Governor of Georgia

Answer: D

Explanation: Thomas Jefferson was the Governor of Virginia, and he was the author of the Declaration of Independence.

QUESTION 21

Which of the following issues did not result in a major compromise at the first Constitutional Convention?

    A. determining state representation in Congress
    B. separating the powers of the central government
    C. determining trade authority for Congress to regulate
    D. allowing slaves to be counted in state's population

Answer: B

Explanation: The issue that did not involve a major compromise was whether to separate the powers of the central government.

QUESTION 22

The Great Compromise, the Three-fifths Compromise, and the Commerce and Slave Trade Compromise were all compromises at the _____.

    A. signing of the Constitution
    B. Constitutional Convention of 1787
    C. Constitutional Convention of 1836
    D. signing of the Bill of Rights

Answer: B

Explanation: The Great Compromise, the Three-fifths Compromise, and the Commerce and Slave Trade Compromise were all compromises at the Constitutional Convention of 1787.

QUESTION 23

    I.   Federalists founded by Alexander Hamilton and John Adams
    II.   Democratic Republicans founded by Andrew Jackson and Martin Van Buren.
    III.   National Republicans founded by John Quincy Adams and Henry Clay.

Of the above, which of the following is an inaccurate statement?

    A. I only
    B. II only
    C. I and II
    D. I and III

Answer: B

Explanation: Thomas Jefferson and James Madison founded the "Democratic Republicans". Andrew Jackson and Martin Van Buren founded the "Democrats".

QUESTION 24

What power is only exclusive to the Legislative Branch?

    A. impeachment power
    B. implement laws
    C. declare war
    D. interpret the law

Answer: A

Explanation: The legislative branch, including both the Senate and the House, is given exclusive powers by the Constitution. The authority to charge the President and other "civil officers" with unlawful activity, is given to the House. A simple majority vote can impeach an elected official.

QUESTION 25

Which of the following is the main purpose of the Lewis and Clark expedition?

  A. find land to eventually find gold
  B. find a waterway from the US to the Pacific Ocean
  C. find land to establish settlement
  D. find a route for the Native Americans

Answer: B

Explanation: One of the goals of Lewis and Clark expedition was to find a waterway from the US to the Pacific Ocean.

QUESTION 26

How did the Louisiana Territory of the Louisiana Purchase protect the nation's trade?

  A. The United States controlled all trade coming in and out of the Port of New Orleans.
  B. It kept the port out of the hands of foreign power.
  C. The United States could cut off access to the port any time.
  D. All of the above

Answer: D

Explanation: The Port of New Orleans was an important port for economic growth and trade. After the Louisiana Purchase, the United States controlled all trade coming in and out of the port. Also, with the Louisiana Purchase, Jefferson kept the port out of the hands of a foreign power that could cut off access at any time.

QUESTION 27

Which of the following United States government policies was a direct consequence of the Trail of Tears of 1838?

    A. taking Native American lands east of the Mississippi River
    B. adding taxes to Native American lands east of the Mississippi River
    C. stopping Native Americans from gaining lands with value
    D. restricting Native Americans from moving

Answer: A

Explanation: In 1838 and 1839, as part of Andrew Jackson's Indian removal policy, the Cherokee nation was required to relinquish its lands east of the Mississippi River and force to move to an area in present-day Oklahoma. This journey was known as the "Trail of Tears," because of its devastating effects.

QUESTION 28

Women's work both inside and outside the home was impacted the most by which of the following technological advances of the Industrial Revolution?

    A. the mechanization of weaving and spinning
    B. the invention of the phone
    C. the invention of the steam engine
    D. the invention of the sewing machine

Answer: A

Explanation: The mechanization of the spinning process was instrumental in the growth of the machine tool industry, enabling the construction of larger cotton mills. Mills generated employment, providing opportunities and incomes to women.

QUESTION 29

Which of the following was Jackson's solution to white settlers' hunger for land?

    A. Northwest Ordinance
    B. Indian Removal Act
    C. Land Removal Act
    D. Westward Expansion Act

Answer: B

Explanation: The Indian Removal Act was signed into law by President Andrew Jackson authorizing the president to trade unsettled lands west of the Mississippi in exchange for Indian lands within existing state borders.

QUESTION 30

Which of the following is inaccurate regarding the Bill of Rights?

    A. The amendments were written part of the original Constitution.
    B. The amendments give rights such as freedom of speech and religion.
    C. Many states refused to accept the Constitution without the Bill of Rights.
    D. The Bill of Rights is an evergreen aspect of the Constitution.

Answer: A

Explanation: The Bill of Rights were the first ten amendments to the Constitution. Those amendments were not a part of the original Constitution that was written.

QUESTION 31

Which of the following indicates that the government may do only those things that the people have given it the power to do so?

    A. limited government
    B. checks and balances
    C. popular sovereignty
    D. separation of power

Answer: A

Explanation: Limited government is a government where any more than the minimal governmental intervention in personal liberties and the economy is not allowed by law.

QUESTION 32

Which of the following amendments gave women the right to vote?

    A. 13th amendment
    B. 15th amendment
    C. 16th amendment
    D. 19th amendment

Answer: D

Explanation: Ratified on August 18, 1920, the 19th Amendment to the United States Constitution granted American women the right to vote—a right known as woman suffrage.

QUESTION 33

Which of the following best describes a major effect of Neolithic agricultural revolution?

    A. additional religious groups forming
    B. the establishing of permanent settlements
    C. equal distribution of wealth
    D. additional military resources

Answer: B

Explanation: With wide-scale transition from a lifestyle of hunting and gathering (moving around to find food) to one of agriculture (settling down to grow food), Neolithic agricultural revolution established permanent settlements.

QUESTION 34

      I.   Pakistan
      II.   Bangladesh
      III.   Malaysia
      IV.   Singapore

When India split into three parts what were the names of the other two parts?

A. I and II
B. I and III
C. II and III
D. II and IV

Answer: A

Explanation: The Partition of India resulted in the regions of India, Pakistan, and Bangladesh.

QUESTION 35

Which of the following events did not contribute to Cold War tensions?

A. United States support to provide food to the citizens of Berlin
B. the establishment of the North Atlantic Treaty Organization
C. rejection of the Treaty of Versailles by the Senate
D. significant economic support for western Europe due to the Marshall Plan.

Answer: C

Explanation: The Treaty of Versailles was one of the peace treaties at the end of World War I. The Treaty of Versailles ended the war between Germany and the Allied Powers.

QUESTION 36

What case did Brown v. Board of Education overturn the ruling of?

    A. Dredd Scott
    B. United States v. Lopez
    C. Plessy v. Ferguson
    D. West Virginia State Board of Education v. Barnette

Answer: C

Explanation: Brown v. Board of Education of Topeka, (1954), was a Supreme Court case ruling that state laws establishing separate public schools for black and white students to be unconstitutional. Plessy v. Ferguson, (1896), was Supreme Court case ruling upholding the constitutionality of state laws requiring racial segregation in public facilities under the doctrine of "separate but equal".

QUESTION 37

Which Constitutional amendment was intended to protect the rights of the newly freed slaves?

    A. 13th Amendment
    B. 14th Amendment
    C. 15th Amendment
    D. 16th Amendment

Answer: B

Explanation: On July 9th, 1868, the 14th Amendment to the Constitution was ratified. The Amendment granted citizenship to "all persons born or naturalized in the United States". This included former slaves recently freed.

QUESTION 38

During the Reconstruction Period, literacy tests and poll taxes were used primarily due to the implementation of which of the following amendments?

    A. 13th Amendment
    B. 14th Amendment
    C. 15th Amendment
    D. 16th Amendment

Answer: A

Explanation: The 15th Amendment gave African American men the right to vote by declaring that the "right of citizens of the United States to vote shall not be denied or abridged by the United States or by any state on account of race, color, or previous condition of servitude." During the Reconstruction Period, literacy tests and poll taxes were used primarily to prevent black from voting.

QUESTION 39

Which of the following civilization was first associated with the concept of democracy?

    A. Greeks
    B. Incans
    C. Egyptians
    D. Romans

Answer: A

Explanation: Athenian democracy developed around the fifth century B.C. in the Greek city-state of Athens. This was the first known democracy in the world.

QUESTION 40

Of the following, which best describes the preamble of the United States Constitution?

   A. purpose of government
   B. summary of the Constitution
   C. limitation of government
   D. distribution of power

Answer: C

Explanation: The preamble states the following: "We the People of the United States, in Order to form a more perfect Union, establish Justice, insure domestic Tranquility, provide for the common defence, promote the general Welfare, and secure the Blessings of Liberty to ourselves and our Posterity, do ordain and establish this Constitution for the United States of America." It is establishing justice, insuring domestic tranquility, protecting welfare, and securing liberty, which all indicates that the government is limited within its powers. This prevents a tyrant government from being established.

QUESTION 41

Of the following, who is considered the principal author of the United States Constitution?

   A. Thomas Jefferson
   B. James Madison
   C. John Adams
   D. George Washington

Answer: B

Explanation: James Madison is considered the principal author of the United States Constitution.

QUESTION 42

How is a political map different than a physical map?

    A. They are exactly the same.
    B. One is a globe while the other is actually a map.
    C. A political map always pretends to be 3D whereas a physical map never pretends to be 3D.
    D. A political map focuses on boundaries and a physical map focuses the geography of the area

Answer: D

Explanation: A political map focuses on boundaries and a physical map focuses geography of the area.

QUESTION 43

According to the idea of supply and demand, a decrease in production rates of oil will mostly likely result in _____.

    A. increase in oil prices for consumers
    B. increase in stock prices
    C. increase in wages
    D. increase in capital investment

Answer: A

Explanation: If production rates of oil are decreasing, then there will be less oil. Therefore, the cost of the price of oil for consumers will increase.

QUESTION 44

Which of the following is the best tool for teaching students the geographic concept of hemispheres?

    A. two-dimensional maps
    B. three-dimensional maps
    C. geography textbook
    D. positioning machine

Answer: B

Explanation: The question ask about teaching the concept of hemisphere, which is a 3D object/concept. The best way to teach is using a three- dimensional map.

QUESTION 45

Which of the following countries is least self-sufficient in regards to natural resources needed for modern industry?

    A. United Kingdom
    B. France
    C. Japan
    D. United States

Answer: C

Explanation: Japan imports almost all raw materials for its industrial economy.

QUESTION 46

High population density along coastlines and early settlement best contributed to which of the following?

    A. larger habitat for animals
    B. access to trade routes
    C. increase communication
    D. increase building construction

Answer: B

Explanation: With high population density along coastlines, early settlers were able to establish access to trade routes. Trade was a critical activity for success of early settlements.

QUESTION 47

A company is introducing a new product line globally. The information initially travels through a process known as:

    A. culture diffusion
    B. contagious diffusion
    C. hierarchical diffusion
    D. movement diffusion

Answer: C

Explanation: Hierarchical diffusion is the spread of ideas that first start in larger cities and then follows to other smaller cities.

QUESTION 48

Which of the following religions did not originate in eastern Mediterranean?

- A. Judaism
- B. Christianity
- C. Islam
- D. Buddhism

Answer: D

Explanation: Eastern Mediterranean is the culture hearth for Judaism, Christianity, and Islam.

QUESTION 49

How do earthquakes create mountain ranges?

- A. collision of continental plates at fault zones
- B. erosion of the earth
- C. distribution of forces during earthquakes
- D. the range difference in elevation

Answer: A

Explanation: An earthquake occurs when two continental plates collide. When those plates collide, they push into each other forcing material to be folded up into huge mountain ranges.

QUESTION 50

Which of the following is a major sociological difference between postindustrial and preindustrial societies?

    A. people are less likely to discuss religion in preindustrial society
    B. people are more focused on oneself than others in preindustrial society
    C. social status is likely to be decided by nonmonetary standards in preindustrial society
    D. women were more involved in business discussions in preindustrial society

Answer: C

Explanation: There was an increase in wealth after the Industrial Revolution, which causes social status to be linked to money. Prior to that (preindustrial society), social status was not linked to money.

QUESTION 51

Which of the following would be considered a primary source for a research project about World War II?

    A. an encyclopedia article
    B. a letter written by a soldier to his brother during the war
    C. a biography of a prominent Union general during the war
    D. a novel set in northern Virginia that takes place during the war

Answer: B

Explanation: A letter written by someone involved during World War II is considered to be primary source.

QUESTION 52

While conducting research on United States politics of the late nineteenth century, a historian considers consulting the autobiography of a prominent politician who was alive in the late nineteenth century. Doing so is most likely to help the historian

- A. to evaluate the long-term consequences of decisions made in the late nineteenth century.
- B. to determine the exact sequence of events.
- C. to obtain insight into contemporary values and beliefs.
- D. to give perspective of individuals' feeling in the late nineteenth century.

Answer: C

Explanation: The historian is looking into politics of the late nineteenth century and consults an autobiography of a prominent politician who was alive in the late nineteenth century. The historian is getting current (contemporary) information about values and beliefs.

QUESTION 53

The Federalist Paper is historically most relevant for which of the following?

- A. foundation for writing the Constitution
- B. foundation for the Bill of Rights
- C. foundation of the analysis and explanation of the Constitution
- D. foundation for the Declaration of Independence

Answer: A

Explanation: The Federalist is a set of 85 articles and essays written by James Madison, Alexander Hamilton, and John Jay endorsing the ratification of the United States Constitution.

QUESTION 54

Which of the following is the best reason for why few bills become laws?

    A. the bill is written poorly
    B. the process is too long
    C. there are many opportunities to terminate a bill
    D. president has the power to veto

Answer: C

Explanation: During the processes to get bills into laws, there are multiple opportunities to terminate a bill.

QUESTION 55

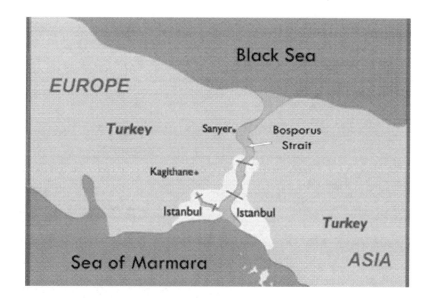

Istanbul's relative location, which is shown on the maps, contributes to controlling which of the following?

A. river
B. ocean
C. strait
D. marsh area

Answer: C

Explanation: A strait is a naturally formed, typically navigable waterway that connects two larger bodies of water. Shown is the Bosporus Strait, which connects the Black Sea to the Sea of Marmara.

This page is intentionally left blank.

PRAXIS® 5004 Social Studies Elementary Education
PRAXIS® II – Elementary Education Multiple Subjects Exam 5001

Made in the USA
Lexington, KY
10 August 2016